KINDLE FIRE HD 8 OWNERS MANUAL

A Visual Owner's Guide on How to Set-Up Your Kindle Fire Device, Including Tips and Tricks to Unleash The Full Potentials of Your Tablet in 5 Minutes, 2019 Updated

ADAMS BOSS
Copyright©2019

COPYRIGHT

TABLE OF CONTENT

CHAPTER 1

INTRODUCTION

The kindle Fire HD 8 is one of the trending tablets of Amazon, it is a device that everybody should get as it very helpful at places of work, our homes and even while travelling.

However, the Kindle Fire HD 8 has a good user interface with a speed that blows your mind, before you can explore the Fire HD 8, you will need to register it on Amazon, and only then you can explore the full capacity of the Kindle Fire HD 8, such as viewing the e-books you bought, read books online, browse, watch videos or music and lots of other interesting things.

CHAPTER 2

HOW TO SET UP YOUR KINDLE FIRE HD 8

To set up the kindle Fire HD, a Wi-Fi network connection is needed, to ensure that your Fire HD is registered, follow the steps below.

Firstly, power up the kindle and connect or click on the available wi-fi network and input the password if the network requires you to do so and proceed.

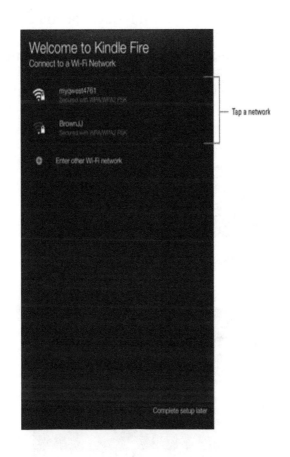

Welcome to Kindle Fire
Connect to a Wi-Fi Network

myqwest4761
Secured with WPA/WPA2 PSK

BrownJJ
Secured with WPA/WPA2 PSK

Enter other Wi-Fi network

Tap a network

Complete setup later

Secondly, the next page will request of you to

input Amazon account information to login but if

you do not have an Amazon account you should

tap on the Create account link to register.

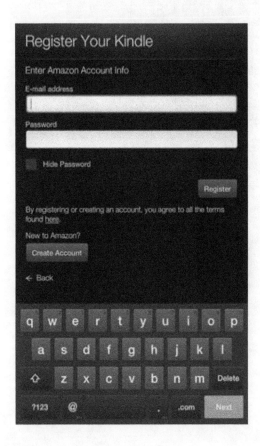

For those who do not have Amazon account, on clicking Create Account this page below will appear and then you can fill in the information required, confirm that they are correct and select "Create Account" and then "Continue" to proceed to the next step.

In addition, you will be given an option to connect to other Social Networks like Facebook and Twitter. To do this, simply tap on the Social Network you wish to connect to and proceed.

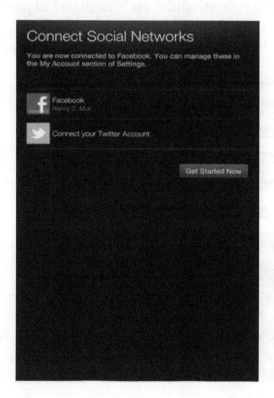

Here you are almost done with registering you Kindle Fire HD 8, several features will appear for you to explore, to enjoy those features, simply click on "Get Started" link and explore your Fire HD.

CHAPTER 3

HOW TO MAKE YOUR E-BOOK APPEAR UNDER BOOK FOLDER IN YOUR KINDLE DEVICE

You can make you e-books to show on your Fire

HD with the cover on the screen. This can be

done with the aid of a e-book converter (Calibre)

on your computer. Launch the application, select

the e-book you wish to convert and click on

convert books.

Next, ensure that the output format is at MOBI

when the convert windows comes up.

Next, select MOBI output on the screen and wipe

out or clear [PDOC] in the Personal Doc tag filed

and select OK to convert your book

At the completion of the converting process, you should make use of a USB cable to transfer your e-books to the BOOK folder of your Kindle Fire HD and make sure the books are showing there.

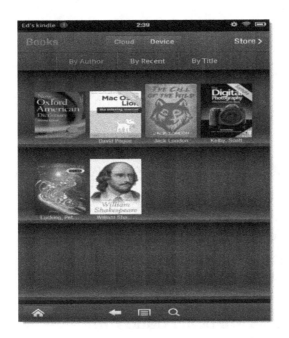

CHAPTER 4

TIPS AND TRICKS EVERY OLD OR NEW KINDLE OWNERS MUST KNOW

Kindle Fire HD8 is one of the best tablets anyone can own, it has a smart user interface and lots of things can be done using it when connected to an internet. However, mastering the operations of your Kindle Fire HD 8 & 10 is something everybody needs; getting an insight of how some tricks are being done with these amazing tablets can be fun.
A lot of people are unaware of these tips and tricks that can be done with Kindle Fire HD 8 & 10, some of which you are to learn from this guide are;

1. How to hard and soft reset your Kindle Fire HD

2. How to enable debugging on your Kindle Fire HD 8 & 10

3. How to bookmark books pages on your Kindle Fire HD 8 & 10

4. How to highlight text in books and add notes

5. How to clear browser history, cookies and cache.

6. How to adjust volume

7.   How to enable or disable your screen rotation

8. How to enable or disable auto-correction and capitalization

CHAPTER 5

HOW TO EASILY HARD AND SOFT RESET YOUR KINDLE FIRE DEVICE

Sometimes your experience some problems with your Kindle Fire HD 8 & 10 devices; and you are faced with the option of resetting it. The step to take is so easy!
 How to Hard Reset
Hard resetting your Kindle Fire device will take it back to the default settings and wipe off all data from the memory.
1st and 2nd Generation Model of Kindle Fire

1. Navigate to "Settings"

2. Click "More"

3. Click "Device"

4. Click "Reset to Factory Defaults"

5. Click "Erase everything"

3rd to 5th Generation Model of Kindle Fire
1. Navigate to "Settings"

2. Click "Devices Options"

3. Click "Reset to Factory Defaults"

4. Click "Reset"

How to Soft Reset
When you soft reset your Kindle Fire, it will only restart your device without affecting or wiping off any data.
1st to 4th Generation Model of Kindle Fire(Hd & HDX)
1. Press and hold down "Power Button" for some seconds until your kindle Fire device goes off.

5th Generation Model of Kindle Fire (HD 8 & 10)

   1. Press and hold down "Power Button" for some seconds until your Kindle Fire device goes off.

CHAPTER 6

HOW TO EASILY ENABLE DEBUGGING ON YOUR KINDLE FIRE HD 8 AND 10

When you enable USB debugging on your Kindle Fire device, you can start making use of it with Android development tools. To do this, follow the steps below.

1. Go to "Settings" on your Kindle Fire

2. This step depends on the version of Kindle Fire

   a. Kindle Fire HD>> Click "Security"

   b. Kindle Fire HDX & New Models>> Click "Device" or "Device Options", Hit on the "Serial Number" seven times till "Developer Options" goes unlocked

c. Kindle Fire Original>> ADB is already enabled by default, so no action is required.

3. Select "Developer Options"

4. Click "Enable ADB" to set it on

Configuring your Windows
1. Click and open "Android Studio", select "Configure", hit "SDK Manager"

2. Click on "Tool", and then "Manage Add-on Sites"

3. Click the "User Defined Sites" tab.

4. Click "New"

5. Enter http://s3.amazonaws.com/android-sdk-

manager/redist/addon.xml on the URL field and click "OK"

6. Hit "Close"

7. On "Extras" region, make sure you select "Kindle Fire USB Driver", click "Install x package" button

8. You need to accept the licenses and click "Install"

9. It will take a few seconds for the Android SDK Manager to download, install all the items.

10.   Now connect your Kindle Fire to your PC

11. Hit "OK" on your Kindle Fire to "Allow USB Debugging", and your device should be seen in the windows as "Android Composite ADB Interface"

12. Stop the ADB server using "adb kill-server" command . To see the Kindle Fire listed, use the "adb devices" command

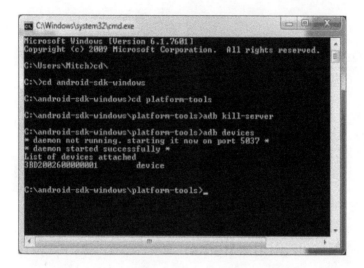

Android development tools on Kindle Fire can be use like DDMS to taki9ng screenshots

Configuring Mac and Linux
1. Connect the Kindle Fire device to your PC

2. Click "OK" on the device and "Allow USB debugging"

3. Stop ADB server making use of "adb kill-server" command.

4. To see your Kindle Fire listed make use of "adb devices" command.

CHAPTER 7

HOW TO EASILY BOOKMARK A BOOK PAGE

When you are reading a favourite book and you want to bookmark that page, follow the instruction below.

1. Click on the screen once and up and bottom frame will show up, you will see the bookmark icon at the top.

Sports Illustrated came to George, who was one of the premier middle linebackers himself, and interviewed George about what he thought of the notion of wiring up Huff for a TV special. George thought for a second and suggested a casting change.

2. Select bookmark and the colour, that means the page has been bookmarked

To access the bookmark follow the instruction below for Kindle Fire HD & HDX...

1. Click the centre of your screen while reading a book.

2. Click "Bookmark"or the bookmark icon

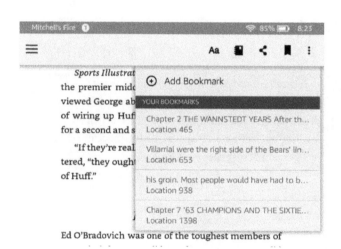

For Kindle Fire 1 versions
1. Click the centre of your screen while reading a book,

2. Click on "Menu" icon at the bottom

3. List of books you bookmarked will appear, Click "My Notes & Marks"

To delete bookmarks, simply access your saved bookmarks using the above step and select "Delete"

CHAPTER 8

HOW TO SIMPLY HIGHLIGHT TEXT IN BOOKS AND ADD NOTES

Just as you can highlight text or passages and add notes in your physical books, you can also do it on Kindle Fire devices. Follow the instructions below to learn.

1. Select and hold the word in the text you want to highlight or add not.

2. It will show you have selected, drag it through other text you want to add.

Golden Age for Nerds. It is our time to THRIVE. You
As a *thriver* (even though that word itself creeps
for some reason)!

As the founder of Nerdism (your new object of worship), I have long been fascinated by productivity and what motivates people to achieve greatness. The Internet is the great equalizer. We all have access to the same data at all times, so there are fewer excuses. How do some people break through while others remain miserable and inert? I ask this question a lot. I have spent even more time trying to ascertain the answer(s).

"Well, who the fuck do you think you are, Chris Hardwick, comedian, former dating show host, current cable host, and pod-caster? Why should I listen to even one crappy word you say?" First off, you're very aggressive. Second, good questions. I have been a lifelong Nerd. As a youth, I was a Nerd

3. To add note, let go of the selected text and a menu will appear.

4. Click "Note" or "Color"/ "Highlight"

and pooped them out into little cubes, with little recourse for pursuing our Nerdly passions in any professional capacity. OUR TIME IS NOW. It's actually *cool* to be *smart*—REWARDED even! It is a

| Note | Highlight | More... |

me out for some reason)! ▼

As the founder of Nerdism (your new object of worship), I have long been fascinated by productivity and what motivates people to achieve greatness. The Internet is the great equalizer. We all have access to the same data at all times, so there are fewer excuses. How do some people break through while others remain miserable and inert? I ask this question a lot. I have spent even more time trying to ascertain the answer(s).

5. Select "Save" in the next windows that will show up.

To access saved notes and highlighted text, click on the centre of your screen and tap "Notepad" icon. For older version of Kindle Fire, click the centre of your screen, and hit the "Menu" icon. This works on Kindle Fire 1&2, HD6, 8 & 10.

To delete notes, click the centre of your screen, click "Notepad" icon for new versions, "Menu" for old versions of Kindle Fire and select the "Trash" icon.

CHAPTER 9

HOW TO QUICKLY CLEAR BROWSER HISTORY, COOKIES AND CACHE

To clear your Silk web browser history, cookies and cache, follow the steps below
For 5th Generation Versions

1. Launch the "Silk" web browser

2. Click on the "Menu" icon at the top left side

3. Select "Settings"

4. Select "Privacy"

5. Select "Clear Browsing Data"

6. Confirm the options you want to delete

   a. "Browsing History"

b. "Cache"

c. "Cookies, Site data"

d. "Save passwords"

e. "Autofill data"

7. Click "Clear" to delete the data from the browser.

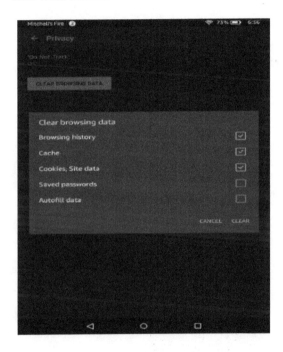

For Older Versions

1. Select "Web" to open the browser

2. Select the "Menu" button at the bottom

3. Select "Settings"

4. Move down and click

   a. "Clear all cookie data"

   b. "Cache"

   c. Clear history"

5. Confirm your delete action by clicking "OK"

CHAPTER 10

HOW TO ADJUST VOLUME EASILY

To adjust the volume of your Kindle Fire, follow the steps below.
For 5th Generation Versions

1. Unlock your screen

2. Press the volume up or down button of your Kindle Fire.

3. Alternatively, go to "Settings", "Sound & Notification", and adjust the "Media Volume" or "Sound Notification Volume".

For Kindle Fire HDX

1. Unlock the screen of your device

2. Press the "+" or "-" button at the back of your Kindle Fire.

For Kindle Fire HD (2nd Generation)
Drag the top bar to access the volume control and drag the slider to adjust the volume.

CHAPTER 11

HOW TO EASILY ENABLE OR DISABLE YOUR SCREEN ROTATION

To learn how to enable or disable auto-rotation of your Kindle Fire screen, follow the instructions below
For Fire HD and HDX,
1. go to menu from the home screen, drag down the bar from the top of the screen.

   For original Kindle fire, click the gear at the top right side of the screen.
2. On new version like HD8 and HD10, hit "Auto-Rotate.

On the old versions, click
"Locked/Unlocked" options. If it shows
"Unlocked" the screen rotation is enabled.

If it says "Locked" the screen rotation is disabled.

CHAPTER 12

HOW TO EASILY ENABLE OR DISABLE AUTO-CORRECTION AND CAPITALIZATION

To learn how to enable or disable auto-correction and capitalization of your Kindle Fire, follow the instructions below. For Kindle Fire HD and HDX

1. Drag down the bar at the top of your Kindle Fire screen

2. Select "Settings"

3. Select "Language and Keyboard"

4. Click "Keyboard Settings"

5. Click "On" or "Off" for Auto-capitalization, and do same to "Auto-correction".

For original Kindle Fire

1. Click on the settings gear

2. Select "More"

3. Select "Kindle Keyboard"

4. Select "On" or "Off" for "Auto-capitalization" or "Quick fixes".

THE END

---

www.ingramcontent.com/pod-product-compliance
Lightning Source LLC
Chambersburg PA
CBHW031232050326
40689CB00009B/1571